CREATIVE GIFT WRAPPING

CREATIVE GIFT WRAPPING

PACKAGE DESIGNS BY
RICHARD KOLLATH

TEXT BY
PHILIPPA KIRBY

PHOTOGRAPHS BY
TONY CENICOLA

Weidenfeld & Nicolson
New York

A FRIEDMAN GROUP BOOK

Copyright © 1987 by Michael Friedman Publishing Group, Inc.

Published by Weidenfeld & Nicholson, New York
A Division of Wheatland Corporation
10 East 53rd Street
New York, New York 10022

Library of Congress Cataloging-in-Publication Data

Kirby, Philippa, 1960-
Creative gift wrapping.

1. Gift wrapping. I. Title.
TT870.K535 1987   745.54   87-13368
ISBN 1-55584-086-8
ISBN 1-55584-087-6 (pbk.)

CREATIVE GIFT WRAPPING: The Complete Guide to Techniques and Ideas
was prepared and produced by
Michael Friedman Publishing Group, Inc.
15 West 26th Street
New York, New York 10010

Editor: Nancy Kalish
Art Director: Mary Moriarty
Photo Editor: Philip Hawthorne
Production Manager: Karen L. Greenberg

Typeset by Lettering Directions
Color separations by Hong Kong Scanner Craft Co. Ltd.
Printed and bound in Hong Kong by Leefung-Asco Printers Ltd.

First edition 1987

10 9 8 7 6 5 4 3 2 1

ACKNOWLEDGMENTS

Our appreciation and thanks to Harry Dennis, Barbara Miller of Hallmark Cards, Inc., Susan Rosenthal of The Stephen Lawrence Co., Ed Gilles and Alan Smith of Contempo, Donna Lichtenstein of Fiber Craft, Elli Schneider of Offray Ribbons, Bill Miller of Ribbon Narrow, Sonnie Levin of Balloon City, USA, and Carolyn and Stephen Waligurski of Hurley Patentee Manor for their generosity and kind support.

CONTENTS

CHAPTER ONE

BASIC TECHNIQUES

Your choice of paper, ribbon, and trimming for a particular gift can be influenced by a number of things: the person for whom you are wrapping, the gift you are giving, and, most of all, the occasion for giving. For example: The red and green paper you use at Christmas will look inappropriate for a July birthday. Think about the occasion you are wrapping for—there is no reason for you to stick to the age-old customs if you do not want to, but those old associations can often act as great jumping-off points. But before addressing the specifics of papers, ribbons, and trinkets, a few wrapping basics have to be understood and mastered.

To start with, the best kind of wrap, regardless of the paper and ribbon you decide to use, should look clean and seamless. This does not mean that you have to apprentice with a department store professional. It just means that you have to allow yourself time to master easy basics. You also have to want to create the perfect wrap—and to allow yourself a smile and a pat on the back when you do!

There are two ways to wrap a uniform, rectangular box: the traditional Seamless Wrap and the double-duty Keepsake Wrap. The Seamless Wrap works best with paper, while the Keepsake Wrap works beautifully with cloth and particularly fine paper. You should make a point to use both wraps, since each has a feel all its own.

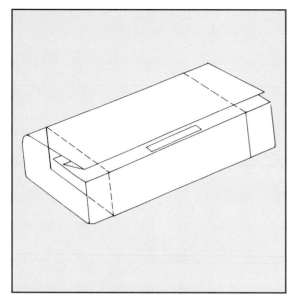

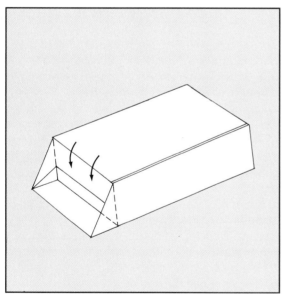

The Seamless Wrap

The Seamless Wrap is a classic. Nine easy steps make this wrap look professional, not to mention irresistible!

1. Estimate how much paper you will need by placing your box on the paper and loosely covering it, as if you were going to wrap it. Overcompensate with the paper; you can always trim off excess, but you will be stuck if you have cut too little paper.
2. Put the paper, "right" side (or face) down, on a flat surface. Next, put the box, top side down, on the paper, with one of its long ends about 2 inches (5 centimeters) from one of the paper's short ends.
3. Make a shallow fold in the other short end of the paper so that an inch (2½ centimeters) of the paper's right side is showing.
4. Now wrap the paper around the box. Run the paper edge with the fold along one of the box's long edges so that the edge is flush with the fold. This point is crucial in creating a seamless wrap. It is worth it to keep adjusting the paper fit around the box until it is exact, so that you really do not have a visible seam. You may

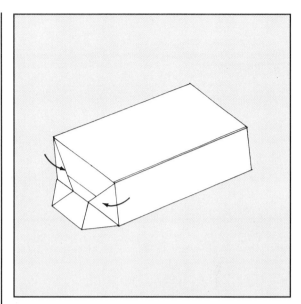

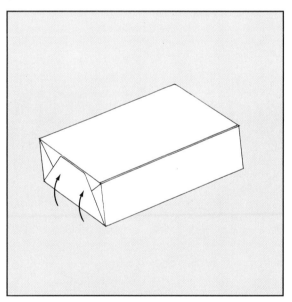

have to do further adjusting if the paper has an obvious pattern; if the pattern is subtle, though, do not try to bully the paper into doing what you want. The paper will be open at both short ends of the box.

5. Tape the long seam with transparent or double-sided tape, running the tape the length of the package. This way, you avoid the possibility of tearing the paper at the tape edges, and you also present an absolutely clean seam.

6. Cut the paper on both open ends so that the paper sticks out 1½ times the height of the box. On one end, fold the top down so you have two paper triangles sticking out on the sides, and sharply crease the edges of those triangles.

7. Fold both side triangles in toward the box.

8. Fold up a lip (half the height of the box) on the raw paper edge. Then fold the paper at the base of the box and bring it up so that the folded edge is absolutely flush with the top of the box, adjusting the fold, if necessary. Tape the length of the seam, using either transparent or double-sided tape. (Again, you should take the time to adjust the paper if it is not flush at first.)

9. Repeat Step 8 on the opposite end.

The Keepsake Wrap

This wrap, which can be done with either fancy paper or fabric, turns a plain box into a gift of its own. The top and bottom of the box are wrapped separately, then held together with a ribbon. The recipient simply takes the ribbon off the box to get at the present—no paper is torn or discarded.

1. To begin, place the bottom half of the box on your paper or fabric, which should be face down on the working surface.
2. Pull up enough paper or fabric to cover both of the longer sides of the box, and allow enough excess to overlap into the inside of the box by 1½ inches (4 centimeters).
3. Cut the paper or fabric and bring up both sides. Lightly tape the paper or fabric to secure the ends to the inside of the box, but only as a temporary measure.
4. Now trim and fold the ends, or shorter sides, keeping enough paper or fabric to overlap the top edge with the same proportion as the side. Tape lightly to secure.
5. When all the sides have been pulled into the interior of the box, you may make any adjustments in smoothing and tightening the sides of the paper or fabric. After this has been done, use double-sided tape (for paper) or a thin layer of white glue (for fabric) to secure the covering to the box surface.
6. Repeat this whole process to wrap the top of the box. You should end up with a wrapped box with a removable top.

You now have a box that can double as a container for all kinds of bits and pieces, long after the gift has been opened and enjoyed

These are the basics. You can adapt these two methods to wrap any rectangular or square-shaped box.

CHAPTER TWO

PAPER

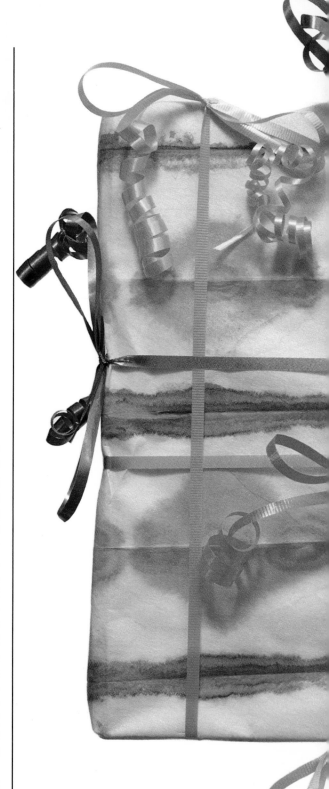

P aper is the basis of any wrap. Even if you decide to create a very complex bow, you have to put that bow on a paper. Card stores are not the only place to look when you are tracking down the perfect wrapping material. You can find papers and fabrics to suit every requirement in all kinds of places. Your hunt can take you to variety stores, craft stores, art supply stores, fabric stores, hardware stores, and florists. You can also take plain paper and pattern it yourself to suit an occasion or a particular person. There are just two things you have to remember: do not limit yourself and have fun!

Tie-dyed paper is easy and very satisfying to make. Go to an art supply store and buy plain rice paper and two colors of India ink. Most art supply stores have a wide variety of rice papers, but for tie-dying, you need an unpatterned, neutral paper. You <u>must</u> use rice paper, because it is very absorbent and will "take" the ink. Conventional wrapping paper just is not absorbent enough.

When you choose your ink, pick colors that complement each other. You can use just one color if you prefer, but you will find it difficult to work with more than two colors. You will need two small watercolor paint brushes as well.

Fold up the sheet of rice paper, accordion style, so that the paper is about 1 inch (2½ centimeters) wide. Place it on a surface that is protected with brown paper bags or on a clean kitchen table or counter. Never use newspaper since the newspaper ink will transfer to your tie-dye.

Pour each ink into a shallow bowl. Dip a paint brush into one of the inks. Run the wet brush the length of one of the long paper edges. Remember that the idea is not to have just a stripe of color, but to have textured, uneven paint patterns. The rice paper will help you to some extent, because

of the way it absorbs moisture, but you need to help nature along a little bit, too, with wavy lines, blobs, and bulges along the edge. When you have painted the paper edge, put the brush aside and use your fingers to press the paint into the paper the entire length of the edge.

Repeat this procedure on the same side until the paper is saturated—about four applications. As the last layer of ink, you may want to use dabs of the contrasting ink on top of the first ink. This adds complexity to the patterns you are making. Allow the paper to dry for fifteen minutes.

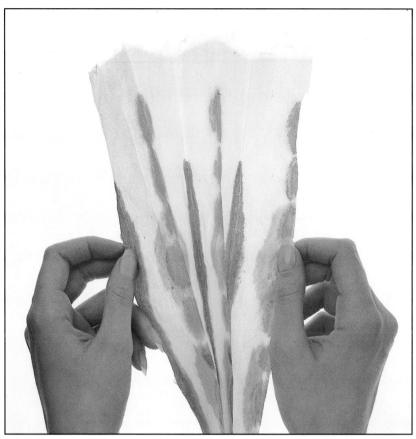

Repeat the process on the paper's other long edge. Again, allow it to dry thoroughly for fifteen minutes. Now, very carefully, unfold the paper, and on a clean, dry surface, smooth out the paper with your hands. And there you are—a truly unique paper!

Wrap a box with your tie-dyed paper, using the Seamless Wrap (see page 12). Find curling ribbon that picks up your ink color (in this case, an orange, two pinks, and a purple) and make a random number of knotted loops around the box as shown in the photograph. Leave long ends for curling. Wrap the ribbon lengthwise and widthwise, but do not use the same piece of ribbon to do both. Each loop should be independent of all the others.

As you make your loops, run the ribbons over and under the other ribbons in a haphazard way. This will give your wrap a loose, woven look.

Ribbon curling is the finishing touch (see page 41). Make some tight curls, some loose curls, and some simple bows in a bunch of vivid colors. All of this variety creates a related and attractive look—it is almost a pity to give this away!

Y ou can make a small keepsake box from scratch to show off a lovely paper, then adorn it with an inventive ribbon treatment. Start with a sheet of stiff cardboard (purchased at a craft store). Cut two cardboard rectangles, each 7-by-5 inches (17-by-12 centimeters). Cut two more rectangles, each 5-by-2 inches (12-by-5 centimeters). Finally, cut two more rectangles, each 7-by-2 inches (17-by-5 centimeters). Using paper packing tape (purchased in variety stores and better card stores), begin attaching the sides. Place one 7-by-5-inch (17-by-12-centimeter) rectangle on a flat surface. Cut a 7-inch (17-centimeter) length of tape, moisten with a sponge (or your tongue!), and slip the tape, wet side up, under one of the 7-inch (17-centimeter) edges, so that half the tape width is under the 7-by-5-inch (17-by-12-centimeter) rectangle. Quickly stand a 7-by-2-inch (17-by-5-centimeter) rectangle, 7-inch (17-centimeter) edge down, on the edge of the 7-by-5-inch (17-by-12-centimeter) rectangle. Do not put the 7-by-2-inch (17-by-5 centimeter) rectangle beside the larger rectangle; you must stand it up perpendicular to and flush along the edge. If you do not do this, your top will have nothing to rest on—it will just fall into the box.

Bring the half width of tape up and stick it to the 7-by-2-inch (17-by-5-centimeter) rectangle to form the back wall of the your box. Repeat the procedure with the other rectangle of the same size; then do the same with the smaller rectangles.

You now have a box bottom. However, you still need to attach the rest of the joints. Tape each larger rectangle to each smaller rectangle along the common 2-inch (5-centimeter) edges with 3-inch (7-centimeter) strips of tape. Flip the extra 1 inch (2½ centimeters) of tape over the top for

reinforcement. Cut 4 2-inch (5-centimeter) tape strips. Before you moisten them, fold them in half lengthwise, with the sticky side out. Moisten. Put each strip along a different 2-inch (5-centimeter) seam on the inside of the box. Repeat this procedure with 2 7-inch (17-centimeter) strips and 2 5-inch (12-centimeter) strips for the inside seams on the box bottom.

Do not worry if the tape is wrinkled or bumpy—you will be able to cover any mistakes with wrapping paper. Cover the box bottom using the Keepsake Wrap technique (see page 14) for box bottoms. Use a piece of paper that is at least 13-by-11 inches (32-by-27 centimeters) in size. Add another inch (2½ centimeters) all around if you are nervous of slips. Cover the top, using the Seamless Wrap (see page 12). When you reach Step 7 of the Seamless Wrap, just fold the triangles flat against the underside of the box top.

When both top and bottom are covered in paper, put the gift inside, surrounded with lots of tissue paper if necessary. Set the covered 7-by-5-inch (17-by-12-centimeter) rectangle on top of the box bottom. And there you have the finished box.

The ribbon used on this box is actually three ribbons on top of one another, tied as if they were just one. Select cloth satin ribbon that complements the paper you have used on your box. Make sure the ribbons are of three graduating widths so you can achieve a layered look. You should have one yard (91 centimeters) of each ribbon. Use tiny pieces of double-sided tape in between the ribbon layers so they do not slide around and ruin the clean line. Loop the ribbon around the box, and tie a bow just below the lid lip on one of the long box sides. Be sure the ribbon is pulled tight enough to prevent the box top from sliding off the bottom. As a final touch, separate the ribbon ends gently.

Different paper textures make for very different looks. Rice paper has a nubby, uneven texture that gives a rustic, country kind of feel. This particular rice paper has flecks of bark in it, and is called mulberry paper. You can buy it at craft stores, along with many other kinds of rice paper. It pays to browse through a few art stores and craft stores to see what is available.

This particular wrap is straightforward—with a twist. Use a Seamless Wrap (see page 12) on your gift. Then make a rice paper band to go around the wrap. It should be slightly less than one-third the width of the box's long sides. Wrap the band around the box and stick down the overlap in the back with transparent tape. This will act as a sort of ruffle, complementing the ribbon.

Use the hemp twine or another natural fiber ribbon that is 4½ times the width of the package. This bow is slightly unusual. Start from the center front of the box, on top of the band, and bring the ribbon back around the box to the front again, forming a loop. Double back to where you began at center front, so that both ribbon ends meet the loop in the front. Then just tie a slip knot to hold the hemp twine on the package. Slip a square of gold origami paper under the knot for contrast.

he world traveler will appreciate this global wrap—and he or she will be able to take it along to hold all those notes and pamphlets picked up along the way. You will need an inexpensive world map, an accordion folder with an elastic band (which you should remove), white glue, a ruler, and scissors.

Put the map, wrong side up, on a clean, flat surface. Place the folder back on the map with the cover flap laid flat. Trace the shape of the whole folder back, including the cover flap, onto the map back. Remove the folder. Then, using the ruler, make a ½-inch (¾-centimeter) border all around the outline, so that you have a new, bigger folder outline.

Repeat this procedure for the folder front, which will be a much smaller rectangle. Create a ½-inch (¾-centimeter) border all around the front as well.

Press out the accordion sides and bottom of the folder. Measure each of the sides with the ruler, and draw three rectangles matching those measurements on the wrong side of the map. Add a border of a ¼-inch (⅗-centimeter) on all sides of the rectangles.

Cut out the folder back, front, sides, and bottom pieces from the map. Glue the back piece to the folder back. Take your time with this by carefully gluing in sections and smoothing down the paper with your hands. Glue the ¼-inch (⅗-centimeter) flaps down. You can make this easier for yourself by cutting a ¼-by-¼-inch (⅗-by-⅗-centimeter) square out of the paper at the two corners. Also, make three small cuts in the paper at the curved folder flap corners. Make a cut on either side of the paper where the folder flap meets the accordian sides between the folder front and back. Allow to dry for ten minutes.

Glue the front map piece to the folder front. Cut squares in the paper at the corners. Glue the ¼-inch (⅗-centimeter) flaps down. Allow to dry.

Last of all, glue the side sections. However, instead of gluing the ¼-inch (⅗-centimeter) flaps as you did with the front and back, you need to fold them under and glue them to the underside

of the paper, except, that is, with the short edges of the bottom piece. Glue these as you did the big pieces. Glue the two side pieces, which are now rectangles with their flaps glued under, to the folder sides. This way, all your edges will be clean with no ragged pieces showing.

Once your box is completed all you have to do is add a broad cloth satin ribbon, tied in an easy bow over the folder cover. Add a touch of whimsy with a tiny flag, toy airplane, car, or pair of sunglasses. And, of course, the greeting card should be a postcard showing a distant land—what better to set the armchair traveler dreaming?

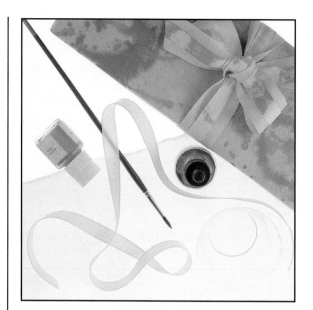

S platter paper is easy to make, and the end results will fool anyone into thinking you used much more effort than you actually did. Start by buying plain white rice paper and two India inks of your choice (all from a craft or art shop). You should also buy cloth ribbon from a fabric store: one plain white grosgrain ribbon and one ribbon that matches one of the inks. Make sure the white ribbon is narrower than the colored ribbon. To apply the ink, you can use either a small watercolor paintbrush or a toothbrush.

Roll out brown paper or other scrap paper on the kitchen table or counter. Place the rice paper on the protected surface. Roll the white ribbon out flat, next to the paper. Put the inks in shallow bowls. Dip the brush into one of the inks and gently pass the brush over the paper, allowing the ink to drip onto the paper. Do not touch the paper with the brush; rice paper is so absorbent, that all you really have to do is drip. If this is the color you want on your ribbon, drip on that too.

When you have dripped one color to your satisfaction, let the paper dry for fifteen minutes. If you are pressed for time, you can speed things up with a hair dryer, on the lowest setting.

Repeat with the second ink color. Allow to dry. The ribbon should be left to dry for one-half hour.

Use a Seamless Wrap (see page 12) with the splatter paper to cover your gift. Then, roll out and center the narrower white ribbon—now splattered—on top of the wider ribbon. Hold in place with tiny pieces of double-sided tape slipped between the two ribbon layers. Wrap the ribbon sandwich around the box in just one direction (not in a cross tie). Tie a conventional bow. Trim the ribbon ends so they are even. And that is it!

This rich, textured paper is a surprise — it is actually a piece of leftover wallpaper! The lovely bow is made from scrap fabric. If you do not have such bits and pieces on hand, take a trip to the fabric store and the hardware store. You are sure to turn up some unexpected treasures. Even if you cannot find something to suit your immediate needs, go ahead and buy scraps, which you will be able to use on another occasion.

Use a Seamless Wrap (see page 12) to cover your gift with the wallpaper. For optimum effect, you should sew your ribbon remnant into a long tube, so you do not have to worry about fraying, or the wrong side showing. If you do not have a sewing machine, you can use some iron-on, double-sided hemming tape (buy this in variety or fabric stores).

To sew up the ribbon, fold the cloth in half lengthwise, with the right sides facing each other. Pin the sides together and sew along one short side and one long side, allowing a ¼-inch (⅗-centimeter) border. Turn right-side out. Turn the cloth in at the remaining open edge. Sew this closed by hand. Press. When you have sewn up the piece of fabric, use it just as if it were ribbon — wrap it around the covered box once, and tie a full bow. Perfect!

ry using unexpected and unconventional materials for wrapping. This gift is wrapped in bubble-wrap, packing material, which you can get in sheets or rolls at office supply, stationery, and better variety stores. Kids especially love this stuff, because each bubble will emit a very satisfying "pop," if pressed long and hard enough. (Of course, this may drive you out of your mind, but that is the price you pay for coming up with such an ingenious wrap!)

First cover your gift with a high-gloss, solid color paper using the Seamless Wrap technique described on page 12. Then wrap over that with the bubble wrap. Cut two extra pieces of bubble wrap, each twice the package length, and use them as ribbon. Tie knots to hold the ribbon in place. Finally, stick something shiny on the middle of the package with double-sided tape—in this case, a square of Mylar was used. And there you have a package guaranteed to please.

S ponge painting paper creates unusual texture. The natural bumps and bubbles of the sponge transfer to the paper surface, and using this technique on shiny paper creates a contrast of matte and glossy that is very pleasing to the eye. This particular wrap combines these elements with colors and a sponge shape that suggests a Native American theme.

Decide what glossy paper you are going to use. Then, buy at least two complementary colors of acrylic paint at an art shop. First wrap your gift with a Seamless Wrap (see page 12). Cut a kitchen sponge into the shape you want with a pair of

kitchen scissors. Pour the first acrylic paint (in this case, white) into a shallow bowl or saucer. Dip the sponge into the paint and blot it gently on a paper towel to remove excess paint. Pat the sponge onto the wrapped package. When you have applied all of the first paint you want, allow the paint to dry for twenty minutes, and wash out the sponge so you can use it for the next paint.

Repeat the steps for the next layer with the second ink (in this case, yellow). Allow the paint to dry another twenty minutes.

The ribbon is the last step. Measure out a piece that is about four times the length of the box. Hemp twine was used on this wrap, picking up the Native American theme of the pattern. Whatever you decide to use, remember that your ribbon should be stiff to achieve this particular look. Lay the box, lengthwise, on the hemp twine. Bring one end up over the box top, down to the opposite box end. Bring the other ribbon end up, just to the top edge. Using the first hemp end (the one that is crossed the length of the box), tie a slip knot. Then, bring the second hemp end up to its opposite box end, twisting it around the first hemp end. Tie a slip knot at the box edge, as you did with the first hemp end. Trim the ends so they stick out about 2 inches (5 centimeters) from the box. What a great wrap!

Here is a wonderful way to create something out of almost nothing. When you really want to have fun with your paper, and you want to make something truly unique, try experimenting with newspaper. You will need spray paint, magic markers, crayons, stick-on stars and bows, and leaves, or other shapes to use as patterns. Anything you want to put on the wrap will work—use your imagination to come up with all sorts of things.

Begin this highly expressive package with a sheet of newspaper wrapped around a box. If you are nervous about soaking through one sheet of newspaper, use two or three sheets to protect your gift. However, one sheet is probably sufficient. Lay leaves on the package top and lightly spray paint around them. Remove the leaves and let the paper dry for a few minutes. Take out the crayons and draw shapes, squiggles, lines, or blobs in different colors. Punctuate the crayon with streaks and dabs of magic marker. Stick down gold and silver stars, then apply bows anywhere you want. The ribbon is a leftover length of silk cord, looped and knotted over the box—but, in keeping with the spirit of the wrap, it rests asymmetrically off to one side. This wrap is especially fun for children to make or receive, and it uses up odds and ends that did not seem to have any purpose. The only limitation on this wrap is your imagination!

CHAPTER THREE

RIBBONS

R ibbons are the absolutely necessary icing on the cake—after all, who wants to look at a cake without icing? Ribbons can be simple, or very elaborate; they can make a stunning statement or quietly complement a vibrant paper.

Basically, there are three different kinds of ribbon that can be used to wonderful effect: curling ribbon, flat satin ribbon, and grosgrain fabric ribbon. Between them, these three kinds of ribbon should meet almost all your wrapping needs.

Try to keep a good selection of ribbon on hand; that way you will be able to handle any gift-giving situation that might suddenly arise (provided that you have a gift to give), and you will also be able to use what you already have as a base when you go out to buy paper or fabric.

Curling ribbon can be purchased in large rolls at variety and card stores. Curling ribbon is usually manufactured in solid colors, but you can get a single roll featuring a number of different colors. You can also buy single color rolls. Unless you know exactly what you want, it is probably better to get the assortment roll—it will see you through emergency situations with ease.

Flat satin ribbon is available in a multitude of widths, colors, and patterns at card and variety stores. Again, try to keep a large roll of assorted colors on hand.

Grosgrain ribbon is wonderful for special wraps—it has a texture and look that are unique. This ribbon, along with other cloth ribbons, is available at fabric stores and in notions departments. Because it is more expensive than curling and satin ribbon, and usually has to be purchased by the yard, you should have a pretty specific idea of how much ribbon you will need before you go shopping.

There are three versatile and attractive bows that will enhance all kinds of wraps. Once you have perfected these, you can adapt them to work well on any gift.

Curling Ribbon Bows

Curling ribbon bows are exuberant-looking and fun to make. But a curling ribbon bow is not just beautiful—it can also cover up any mistakes you might have made in the process of wrapping your gift. Use it on the neck of a wrapped champagne bottle or on the twisted ends of a bonbon-style wrap.

You can estimate how much ribbon you will need by wrapping the ribbon around the box without cutting it. Be generous! Do not tie the ribbon ends in a bow, however. Simply tie a double knot and leave the ribbon ends dangling. Cut six or seven varied lengths of curling ribbon and tie them in the center around the first knot. You should now have about fourteen lengths of ribbon, all tied at the same center point. Grasping one piece of ribbon at a time, as close to the knot as you can, draw the ribbon firmly between a scissor blade and your thumb to form a long corkscrew curl. Repeat the procedure on the same ribbon if you want really tight curls. Do the same with each of the other ribbons. You will now have a springy mass of curls crowning your wrap. If you want greater texture in the bow, try making some of the curls tight and some loose, or leave a couple of tendrils uncurled.

Arcing Bows

Flat satin ribbon lends itself perfectly to sleek and high-tech looks. A subtle arcing bow will add a delicate accent to glossy, unpatterned paper. It is easy to make and looks very professional.

Start by wrapping two separate ribbons around your package instead of one piece that is twisted where the ribbon changes direction. Cut one length of ribbon to wrap all the way around the long end of the box, and another to wrap around the short end. Tape the ribbon to the box bottom where the two loops cross. This approach is smoother than the usual twist and adds to the sleek feel of your wrap.

Using the same color ribbon, cut five lengths for your bow. The ribbon pieces should be about 9½ inches (24 centimeters), 8 inches (20 centimeters), 6½ inches (16½ centimeters), 4 inches (10 centimeters), and 2½ inches (6 centimeters) long, though any lengths using this ratio will work. Make a circle with each ribbon piece, overlap the ends slightly, and tape, using a tiny piece of double-sided tape. Place the taped edge of the largest circle on the cross formed by the ribbon already on the box. Press the circle down in the center with your fingers so that it meets the bottom and forms two little loops.

Proceeding from the larger to the smaller, layer the next three circles on top of the first and press them down in the center, as you did with the first. Add the smallest circle at the end, but do not press it down. You should now have a symmetrical, semicircular bow rising above the box. All the ribbons should be aligned with the flat ribbon on the box.

To attach the bow, you can either staple the loops to the flat ribbon at the cross, or use a needle and thread to make a small stitch.

You can make the arcing bow do double duty by adding more loops and creating a rosette bow. Instead of cutting just one piece of ribbon of each length, cut three or four. As you layer the loops, fan them out to form a full circle on the box. Attach in the same way as the arcing bow.

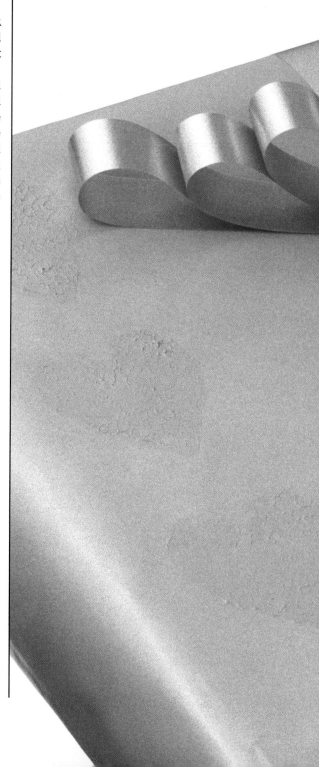

Twist Bows

The softness and richness of grosgrain ribbon can be used to create a wonderful effect with a simple twist bow. This bow is ridiculously easy to make—satisfaction is absolutely guaranteed!

Wrap the ribbon five times around the fingers of your left hand (or right hand, if you are left handed), or around the long side of a piece of cardboard measuring 2-by-6 inches (5-by-15 centimeters). Make a small stitch with a needle and thread, attaching the end of the ribbon to the loop next to it, so that it stays in place. Use tape instead of thread if you are using a non-cloth ribbon. Do not use tape, however, on a cloth ribbon. Make sure the ribbon is lined up around your fingers in one continuous loop. Carefully slip the ribbon off your fingers, maintaining the loop. Folding the loop in half, cut triangle shapes away on both sides of the ribbon in the center, as shown in the photograph. Be very careful not to cut the triangles so large that they meet. If they do, the ribbon will break and the bow will be ruined. Tie the ribbon together at the triangles with a new piece of ribbon. Pull the loops out, one at a time (as shown in the photograph), twisting gently as you pull. Grosgrain ribbon will produce an easy, floppy bow; flat satin ribbon, a full, lush bow.

B lack glossy paper shows off any bow perfectly. The more complex and ornate a bow, the more complementary your paper should be. Because the color of this magnificent harvest bow is gold, black is a dramatic foil.

Fall is the perfect time to make this bow, since ears of dried corn are readily available. Buy three small ears, all about the same size, with their dried husks still attached. Evenly spray paint the ears gold, working with each ear individually. Allow the ears to dry thoroughly. (You should follow the instructions on the paint can, since different paints require different drying times.)

Although the ears are incorporated into the ribbon bow, it is a good idea to use florist's or gardener's wire to attach the ears to each other first. This gives the bow arrangement strength and will save you from worrying that it will come apart before the gift is opened. Wrap the wire several times around the ear where the kernels and husk meet, until they are secure.

Gold mesh ribbon, purchased in a craft store, brings the whole look together. When you have wrapped the gift with the paper, pull the ribbon around it and tie a double knot where the ribbon crosses on the package top. Place the corn bouquet on the knot. Bring the ribbon ends up to tie a conventional bow, making sure the ribbon covers the florist's wire. With the pale gold husks, the gold kernels, and the gold mesh ribbon, you have a bow of wonderful texture and life.

R ibbon does not have to be just pretty and ornamental—it can also perform an important service. This brilliant red cloth ribbon holds these two packages together—in more ways than one! The rich color of the ribbon also contrasts with the patterns and colors of the papers to pull the design together.

Start by wrapping the larger bottom box, using the Keepsake Wrap technique described on page 14. Use a boldly patterned paper on the box bottom, and a more subtle paper on the box top that picks up an essential element of the first paper. The big and little squares of this gift are a great example of flip-flopped shapes, though you might want to try something with polka-dotted paper, or stripes.

Now, using the Seamless Wrap technique (see page 12), cover the smaller box with the same paper you used on the bottom of the first. When you have wrapped it, center the small box on top of the big box. It is a good idea to attach the top box to the bottom box with two small strips of double-sided tape. This will allow you to make a looser bow since the ribbon will not have to be pulled tight to hold the boxes precisely in place.

Last of all, tie a big conventional bow around both boxes. Cut triangular notches in the ends of the ribbon to keep it from unraveling. And there you have it!

Trick the eye by putting three bows where you expect just one. This delicately printed paper is highlighted with three simple satin cloth bows. When you choose the ribbons, use satin cloth ribbon to add lustre and try to pick up a color from your paper. Experiment with various tones and widths. In this case, the brightest color is in the middle with the lighter and darker ribbons on the sides. Make three loops around the box, and tie conventional bows. Notch the ribbon ends to prevent straggling threads. You now have a pretty and unexpected look, with the bows making the real wrap statement.

A full, lush bow can make such an impact that the paper takes second place. This wonderful twist bow (see page 44) uses grosgrain polka-dot ribbon. The bow sits high on the package, acting as a focal point. Texture is added when the ribbon has right and wrong sides; experiment with ribbon that is flat on one side and satiny on the other.

If you are ambitious, you might want to try making the bow with two kinds of ribbon at once. Place two kinds of ribbon back to back and wrap them around your fingers as if they were one. The trickiest part of this bow will be notching the ribbon for the twist. However, this can be done, carefully, layer by layer. As long as you do not accidently cut through the middle of the ribbon, your double-layered bow will work wonderfully. The tangle of loops and color that you will get will be a delight—you may even want to try three ribbons at once!

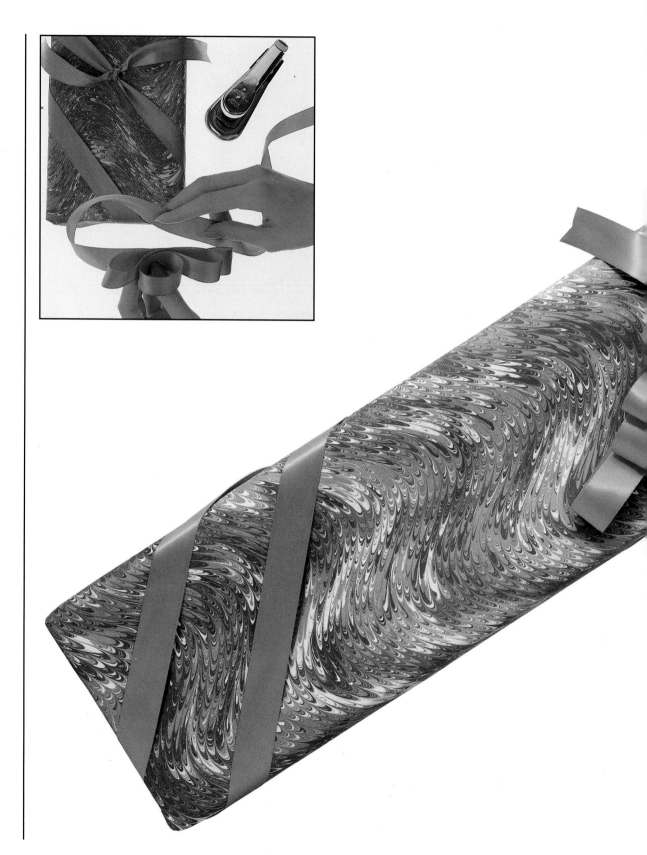

The exuberance of the twist bow would overwhelm a slim and delicate package such as this one. The beauty of the marbleized paper calls for a very different bow effect. In this wrap, the undulations of the paper pattern are picked up by the asymmetrical satin cloth bow, which leaves the paper at the package center visible for admiration.

Instead of making separate loops of ribbon around the wrapped box, wrap one ribbon around the package four times at an angle as shown, and knot on top. Leave the knotted ends dangling, to make a subtle contrast with the pattern lines and the ribbon lines. Make a separate arcing bow (see page 42), using the same ribbon, and attach it to the package at the knot point. Instead of stapling the bow to the ribbon, however, tie it on with the ribbon ends. The bow will probably rest at a slight angle, as it does in this wrap. This is fine—do not force the bow to be straight, since you will only end up with crumpled loops. The result is a delicate look with long, flowing lines.

F or this lively wrap, you should buy an assorted roll of shiny curling ribbon, which you can find at any variety or card store. The tiny, heart-shaped balloons can be purchased in specialty shops.

First, wrap the box in a glossy, bright paper, using the Seamless Wrap. Calculate the length of ribbon you will need for the box strips by wrapping a quantity of ribbon (uncut, and still on the roll) down the height and across the base, back up the height again, and over top of the box, allowing 2 inches (5 centimeters) excess for a knot. Cut it at this point and use it to measure out seven more identical lengths from different colored ribbons.

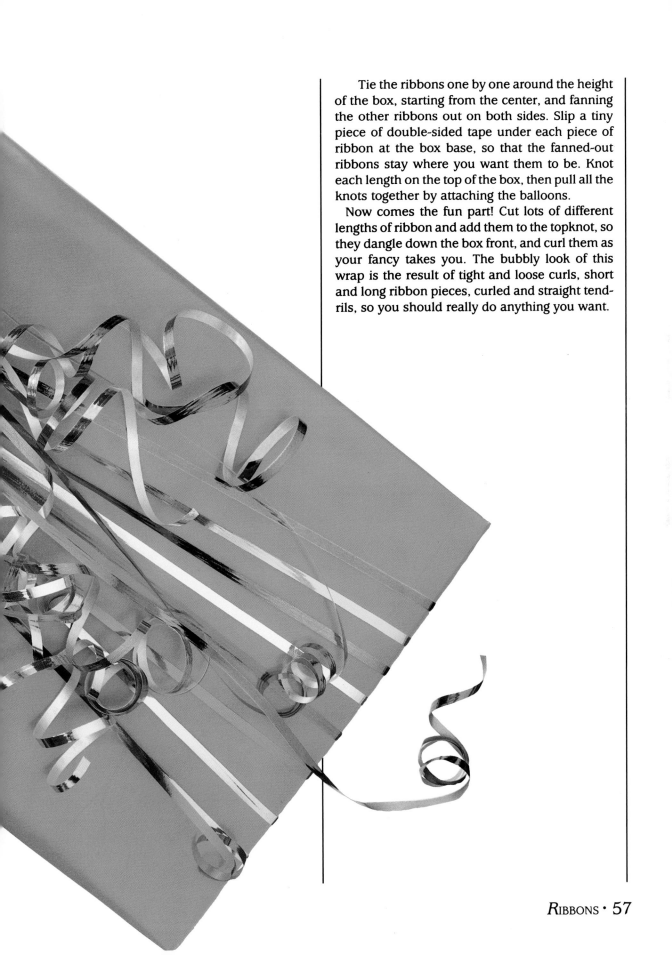

Tie the ribbons one by one around the height of the box, starting from the center, and fanning the other ribbons out on both sides. Slip a tiny piece of double-sided tape under each piece of ribbon at the box base, so that the fanned-out ribbons stay where you want them to be. Knot each length on the top of the box, then pull all the knots together by attaching the balloons.

Now comes the fun part! Cut lots of different lengths of ribbon and add them to the topknot, so they dangle down the box front, and curl them as your fancy takes you. The bubbly look of this wrap is the result of tight and loose curls, short and long ribbon pieces, curled and straight tendrils, so you should really do anything you want.

Even with no time and little effort, you can create a complete and fun wrap like this one. Buy twelve stick-on bows in assorted colors from a variety or card store. Use a paper with a limited pattern—avoid complicated florals or intricate geometrics, since you will find that these designs will compete with the bows for visual attention.

Once you have wrapped your box, start sticking the bows on. Play around a little bit with your bows before you stick them down. The bows in this wrap form a Christmas tree, but, of course, you can fashion any shape you want (though remember to stay with primary shapes, or else the recipient will not be able to guess what you have made). Try making a big star, a sailboat, a flower on a stem, or a car.

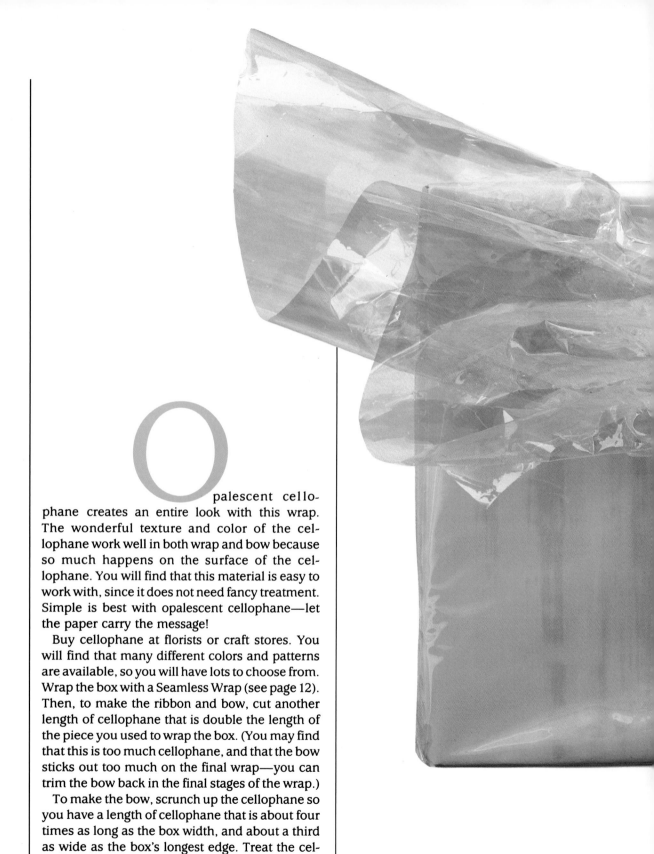

Opalescent cellophane creates an entire look with this wrap. The wonderful texture and color of the cellophane work well in both wrap and bow because so much happens on the surface of the cellophane. You will find that this material is easy to work with, since it does not need fancy treatment. Simple is best with opalescent cellophane—let the paper carry the message!

Buy cellophane at florists or craft stores. You will find that many different colors and patterns are available, so you will have lots to choose from. Wrap the box with a Seamless Wrap (see page 12). Then, to make the ribbon and bow, cut another length of cellophane that is double the length of the piece you used to wrap the box. (You may find that this is too much cellophane, and that the bow sticks out too much on the final wrap—you can trim the bow back in the final stages of the wrap.)

To make the bow, scrunch up the cellophane so you have a length of cellophane that is about four times as long as the box width, and about a third as wide as the box's longest edge. Treat the cellophane length as if it were a ribbon, and wrap it around the box, knotting it on top.

CHAPTER FOUR

SOMETHING SPECTACULAR

Wrapping a gift for someone special, or for a special occasion, lets you play with themes and ideas. Think for a second about the event prompting the gift. Are there traditions that go with the event? Or think about your recipient. Are there ideas or themes you instantly associate with that person?

Gifts for babies make us think of pastel colors and simple shapes. These attractive presents are bright enough to catch any youngster's eye. They are done with stencils, which you can either buy or make yourself.

Have on hand a stencil book, acrylic or stencil paint (in as many colors as your design calls for), a stencil brush or short-bristled oil paintbrush, and an art knife (such as an X-acto), all of which you can buy at art and craft stores.

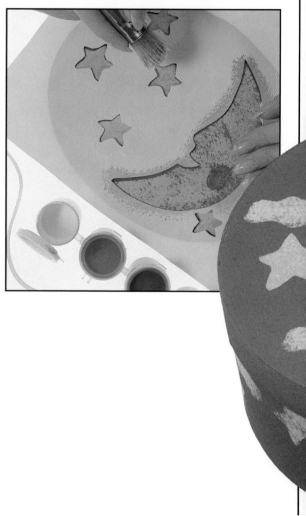

If you desire, however, you can create your own stencil design on cardboard, bought at an art supply store. Draw on the cardboard, then cut out your designs with the art knife. It is best to have a precise idea of the area you want to cover with the stencils so that you can both use a sheet of cardboard that will cover the whole area and be sure the shapes you cut out will all fit on the box top. If you decide to use a book of stencils, follow the instructions in the book.

Once your stencil sheet is done, you are ready to begin. Place the sheet on top of your gift, which has been wrapped with matte, or flat, paper. Using the brush, dab the paint, in sharp jabs, into the holes of the stencil and on the package—do not use a back and forth motion with the brush as you would if you were painting. This technique gives the distinctive show-through look that characterizes this stenciling. When you have filled in the shapes you want with the first color, let the paint dry about fifteen minutes. Wash out the brush and move on to the second color. You can paint over dried paint if you wish, as was done on the packages in the photograph.

You can also stencil the rest of the package, if you wish. When you add the ribbon and bow, you should decide whether you want to let the ribbon interfere with your design, or whether you want it

to stay separate. Both approaches are shown here. Choose a ribbon that picks up one of the colors you have worked with. You may also want to use ribbon that is shiny, as a contrast to the matte colors you have been working with. Cloth satin ribbon works wonderfully, and if you can find one that is as unusual as the sunny yellow ribbon shown here, all the better!

T his powder blue wrap is highlighted not just by the tiny bear, but also by the subtle, sponged hearts. Use a felt-tipped pen to draw a heart on a sponge. Draw the heart near the sponge edge so you cut down on time spent with the scissors—also, you save more sponge for future cutting. Pour pink acrylic paint into a shallow bowl, and sponge heart shapes onto the already wrapped present.

This cheerful package also sports an arcing bow (see page 42) stuck directly onto the paper. Perhaps the most appealing touch, however, is the bear (available in any toy store and in many good card stores). Notice how the blue satin cord bow around his neck is actually what attaches him to the gift. You can use this idea with any other knickknacks you might want to put on a gift—for a child, it might be a rattle or a tiny model car.

Each of the box-es in this wonderful Shaker box pyramid has been textured with paint and a comb. The effect is so delicate and surprising that it makes the boxes look as if they have been covered in moiré silk. Yet you can do it in about a half hour!

Buy three Shaker-style boxes in decreasing size at a craft store. Buy two colors of stencil paint for each box at the craft store, too, bearing in mind that each pair of paints should complement each other. The boxes shown feature light paint on dark paint—pink on red, yellow on orange, and brown on black.

Begin by painting all of one box with the darker base color. Allow to dry about twenty minutes. Using the second paint, paint over the base coat. While the paint is still wet, carefully run a comb over the box in a gently undulating motion. Repeat all over the box. Remember to apply only slight pressure—you want to scrape only the top coat, not the base.

Repeat the procedure for the other two boxes. Then when they are thoroughly dry, fill and stack them. Hold them together with a piece of natural ribbon or twine; these boxes are tied with a length of coconut fiber.

Fun fake fur makes a great sack to put a present in. Buy a ½-yard (45 centimeters) of fake fur at a fabric store, and cut out two rectangles, each measuring 8-by-12 inches (20-by-30 centimeters). Stitch a ½-inch (1¼-centimeter) hem on one of the 8-inch (20-centimeter) sides of each rectangle. Right sides facing, sew the two rectangles together on all but the hemmed sides. Use a running stitch. Turn the sack right-side out, and you have a fabulous fur wrap for frivolous, fun gifts. It is a good idea to pad the sack with lots of tissue paper after placing your gift inside, so the back has a voluptuous, full look. Close the bag with a cloth satin ribbon, secure with a double knot, and finish with a bow. Leave some suggestive corners of the tissue paper poking out to make this wrap unbearably enticing.

ny child with a love of the outdoors or camping, or any young scouts you might know, will like these rustic bandanna wraps. And they are so easy to make!

Place a small boxed gift in the middle of the bandanna so that the box edges form 45-degree angles with the kerchief edges. This means that when you bring the kerchief corners up over the box, the four cloth corners form triangles, rather than squares.

Bring the two opposite triangles together and knot them at the package center. Then bring the other two triangles up and knot them too. The second knot should cover the first knot. Adjust the triangle sides and tuck under as needed. Bear in mind that the size of the bandanna must correspond to the size of the present—so do not think of wrapping a set of encyclopedias this way.

This wrap is a present all by itself! In fact, when the gift has been taken out of the balloon basket, your recipient can hang up the balloon as an original mobile.

For this extremely elegant wrap, you will need a large Styrofoam ball, a wooden Shaker-style box with a lid, white glue, wire cutters, a dull kitchen knife, a ½-yard (45 centimeters) of fabric, three coat hangers, and three different types of ribbon: a narrow satin ribbon for the bows; a wide, flat ribbon for disguising the balloon's mechanics; and a very thin gold tinsel rope. Try to buy the fabric and the ribbon at the same time so you can be sure they will work well together. The same goes for the Styrofoam ball and Shaker box. They should be in the right proportions so that they work as a balloon and basket. Both can be found at crafts stores.

To turn the Styrofoam ball into a balloon, measure out a strip of fabric that is about twice as wide as the ball is high. Using an art knife, score the ball from center top to center bottom along the diameter. Lay the ball on the reverse side of the fabric, and with the dull kitchen knife, push about a ½-inch (1¼ centimeters) of one end of the material into the cut you have already made, following the rounded contour of the ball. Wrap the fabric around the ball to meet with the end already secured in the ball. Allow a ½-inch (1¼ centimeters) of excess and cut the cloth. Press the fabric into the score with the existing material, using the knife. To round off the top and underside of the ball, make cuts in the excess material and push the fabric into the ball. (Do not worry about this too much, since you will be able to cover your mistakes with bows at the end.) Take the coat hangers and cut each one twice—once on each of the short sides, 2 inches (5 centimeters) away from the joint with the long side.

Measure and cut fabric to cover the width of the box base. Do this by rolling the box along the fabric. Start at the edge of the fabric, marking the starting point on the box. Roll the box until you have overlapped the starting point by an inch (2½ centimeters). Cut the fabric. Cover the side of the box with white glue, and apply the fabric, smoothing it out as you go along. While the glue is still wet, pierce the covered box with one end of each of the coat hangers, at three evenly spaced points around the diameter. Allow to dry.

Cover the lid and base of the box by tracing the lid shape onto the reverse side of the fabric and allowing a ¼-inch (⅗-centimeter) all around. Cut both forms out. Cover the top surface of the box with white glue and apply the fabric. Cut small notches into the edge of the remaining fabric, so it will lay smoothly, and glue these to the side of the lid. Repeat this procedure for the box base.

Measure another length of fabric to trim the edge of the box lid by rolling the lid along the wrong side of the fabric (as you did with the box side). Fold the edges under, using white glue to stick them down. Push the angled ends of the coat hangers right through the fabric and into the Styrofoam ball. Trim with the ribbon, which you should first arrange with pins before gluing in place.

T his lovely box uses the same principle of wrapping as the balloon box (see pages 74 to 77). The only difference is that this box does not have wire hangers poked into it. Done with care, this box will have a life after the gift-giving.

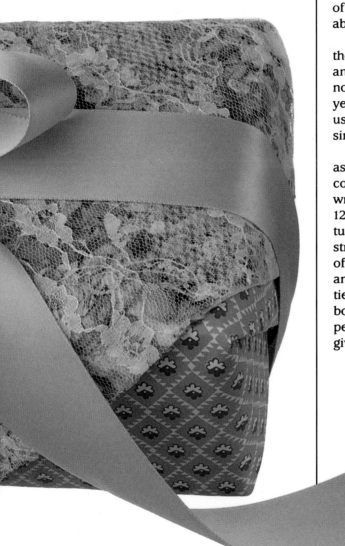

Almost every color you can think of is somewhere in this wrap of potpourri, geometric paper, and ribbon. But the wrap does not seem too busy or confused. The reason for this sense of calm is the presence of a wonderful, warm brown that manages to absorb and combine all the colors.

Start by buying a sheet of potpourri. (Odd though it may sound, this is not an esoteric item, and you will not have trouble finding it, even in nonspecialized craft stores.) If you are not sure yet of the exact dimensions of the box you will be using in the wrap, buy more than one sheet size since you can always find other uses for them.

Use a paper with a small geometric print such as this one. Do not go for a floral print that will compete with the potpourri. When you have wrapped the box with a Seamless Wrap (see page 12), place the potpourri sheet on top of the box, turned so that the four points dangle over the four straight box sides. You may want to slip a couple of pieces of double-sided tape between the sheet and the paper to keep the sheet in place. Finally, tie a traditional cross-type bow with a satin ribbon, and you have finished a romantic wrap, perfect for enclosing a gift at Valentine's or just for giving to someone special.

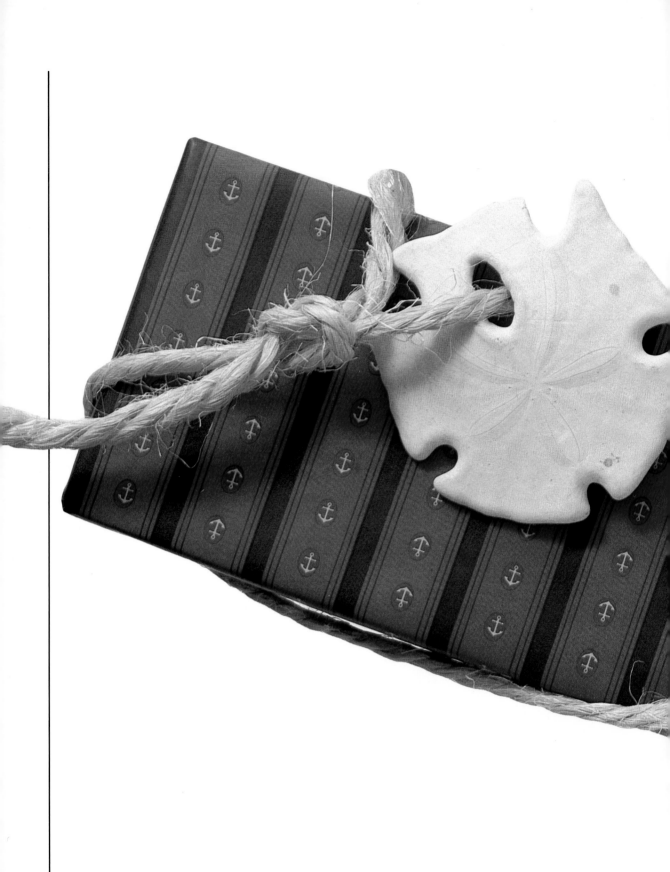

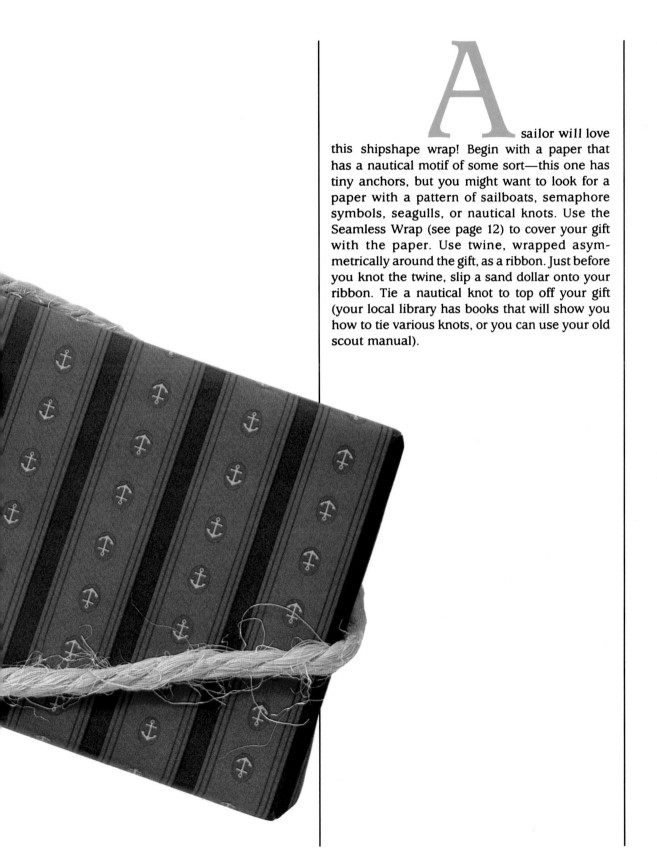

A sailor will love this shipshape wrap! Begin with a paper that has a nautical motif of some sort—this one has tiny anchors, but you might want to look for a paper with a pattern of sailboats, semaphore symbols, seagulls, or nautical knots. Use the Seamless Wrap (see page 12) to cover your gift with the paper. Use twine, wrapped asymmetrically around the gift, as a ribbon. Just before you knot the twine, slip a sand dollar onto your ribbon. Tie a nautical knot to top off your gift (your local library has books that will show you how to tie various knots, or you can use your old scout manual).

A fishing enthusiast or cook will appreciate this amusing wrap. Wrap your gift in a glossy paper using the Seamless Wrap technique on page 12. This lively red will show off your plastic fish to its best advantage.

The green cloth ribbon with white polka dots will attach the fish and add a touch of tongue-in-cheek humor to the gift. Start by looping the ribbon underneath the package at one end and bringing it up over the box top. Lay the fish along the length of the package, with the tail overhanging the package edge by about a ½-inch. (1¼ centimeters). Cross the ribbon over the fish body near the tail. Bring the two ribbon ends under the gift and make another cross, more or less directly under the box center. Hold the fish in place with one hand and turn the package over carefully to make sure the ribbons cross properly on the underside.

Bring the ribbon ends up to the top side again and tie a slightly loose bow. With a finger, push the bow gently into the spot it should logically fall. Pull the fish forward so its nose nudges the bow, holding it in position. Slip three or four small pieces of double-sided tape under the fish to hold it in place. Cut three more tiny pieces of double-sided tape and put one under the crossed ribbons on the box bottom, another under the starting loop under the box, and the last under the bow. Sprinkle sparingly with multicolored confetti, and voilà! This present is a real catch!

An extravagant valentine deserves a beautiful cloth wrap. Follow the principle behind the flat-topped covered box (see page 22) to make this warm and welcoming heart. If you do not feel up to drawing a heart on a sheet of stiff cardboard to make your template, use the bottom of a heart-shaped box of chocolates. Or you can skip making the box from scratch and buy a heart-shaped box at a crafts store to cover with your choice of fabric.

If you do make a box from scratch, first draw a large heart on a sheet of paper. The easiest way to do this is to fold the paper in half and draw a half heart, with the heart's center at the fold. Any child will tell you that the hardest part of drawing a heart is making both sides even. But if you can make a reasonably symmetrical half heart, you will be in business!

When you have cut out the paper template, trace its outline onto the sheet of cardboard. Cut out the cardboard heart. Next, draw a second paper heart that is a ¼-inch (⅗-centimeter) larger than the first on all sides. Trace it onto the cardboard, and cut it out as well. The next step is to figure out how much cardboard and material you will need for the box sides and the rim of the top of the box. To do this, lay a length of string along the perimeter of the smaller cardboard heart. Start at the center top of the heart and bring the string all the way around, back to where you started. Cut the string to this exact length. Then, measure a second piece of string around the perimeter of the larger heart, and cut it to that exact length.

Using tailor's chalk (purchased at a fabric store), trace both hearts onto the wrong side of the material you are using. Measure a ¼-inch (⅗-centimeter) border around all sides of both hearts by hand. Do not worry if the borders look a little shaky; they will not be visible in the final product. Cut out the cloth hearts. Glue the smaller fabric heart to the smaller cardboard heart with a thin, even layer of white glue, making sure that the ¼-inch (⅗-centimeter) border sticks out on all sides. Do the same with the larger fabric and cardboard hearts. Allow to dry for a half hour.

Using the shorter piece of string you cut, measure out one piece of cardboard the same length as the string. Use a ruler to make the line straight. Now, determine how deep you want the box to be—4 inches (10 centimeters) is a good depth—and draw a 4-inch (10-centimeter) line down from both ends of the string length. Join the bases of these 4-inch (10-centimeter) lines to form a very long rectangle. Add a ¼-inch (⅗-centimeter) border on each of the long sides and cut the rectangle out. Use tailor's chalk to trace the outline on your material as you did with the hearts (don't forget the border!).

Repeat this process with the larger piece of string to create the rim of the box top. But instead of drawing 4-inch (10-centimeter) lines, draw ¾-inch (2-centimeter) lines for the correct width of the rim. Continue the same process as outlined above until you have another cardboard rectangle (longer and thinner than the previous one) and a matching piece of cloth.

Find the center of the smaller rectangular piece of cardboard by folding it in half. Place the halfway fold at the point of the smaller heart. Forming the box sides is the trickiest part, and not for the faint-hearted! Holding the center of the rectangle at the point of the heart, shape the rectangle to fit the contours of the smaller heart, gluing the cloth heart border, piece by piece, to the upright cardboard side. This serves to reinforce the wall and base joint, which must be as strong as possible.

When this is done, reinforce the inside of the box side with paper packing tape. Stick this down in 2-inch (5-centimeter) pieces, not in a strip as you would do with a straight-sided box. Be liberal with the tape, and do not worry about any tape wrinkles and bulges, since you can camouflage those later.

Next, find the center of the longer and thinner cardboard rectangle by folding it in half. Place the halfway fold at the point of the larger heart and repeat the process detailed above of fitting it to the contours of the heart. Glue and reinforce it the same way as well.

When this is done, pat yourself on the back! Then, take the smaller cloth rectangle and fold over and glue one of the ¼-inch (⅗-centimeter)

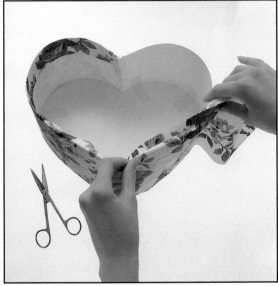

borders running along the length of the rectangle, down on the back of the cloth. Allow the border to dry, pressed under heavy books to weight it down. When dry, find the center of the cloth rectangle as you did with the card, and start gluing it to the box side. The already glued cloth edge should be the edge flush with the box bottom. The other border should stick a ¼-inch (⅗-centimeter) up over the box sides. Make regular vertical cuts in the border. Let the glued cloth dry on the box sides.

Fold each border segment over the edge top and glue down one by one. Let dry. Next, take the longer and thinner cloth rectangle and fold over to the wrong side and iron down (or glue) the ¼-inch (⅗-centimeter) borders running along both long sides. Attach the cloth rectangle to the cardboard rectangle with a thin layer of white glue.

Now all you have to do is fill the box with clouds of tissue paper and a gift, and put the top on. Use red grosgrain ribbon both to trim the box and to hold the top on. Tie a loose bow, and add knots to the ribbon ends for a slightly different look.

The tiny cloth pillow heart is the perfect way to use up scraps left over from the box. It can be filled with potpourri, or anything else you wish to use that is fragrant. To make this heart, use the same procedures you used to make the heart box. Begin with half a heart drawn on a piece of folded paper; cut it out, and trace its shape onto the back of a fabric scrap. Add a ¼-inch (⅗-centimeter) border on all sides. Trace the heart again onto another piece of fabric, adding the border. Cut out both hearts. Put them together, right sides facing each other, and sew them together. You can do this easily by hand if you do not have a sewing machine. Leave an inch (2½ centimeters) unsewn along one of the long edges so you can turn the heart right side out.

When you have finished sewing and the heart is right side out, carefully fill it with the material you have chosen. Sew up the opening as unobtrusively as you can with tiny stitches. To finish off, make a small ribbon bow and stitch it onto the heart. This little sachet can be slipped into a lingerie drawer, or hung in a closet for a breath of fresh air or as a constant reminder of the person who gave the gift.

You do not always
have to devote hours and hours to creating the
perfect wrap. Add a fresh country touch to traditional valentine motifs with red and white gingham ribbon. Start with the reddest, shiniest
paper you can find. Use it to wrap a rectangular
box with a Keepsake Wrap (see page 14). Put two
paper doily hearts on the box top, stuck down
with small pieces of double-sided tape (you can
find the doily hearts at variety stores and card
stores). Pull the look together with two pieces of
red and white gingham ribbon (bought in a fabric
store), tied separately around the box so that the
two bows you make fall right in the center of the
hearts. Notch the ribbon ends to prevent fraying.
If you want to, you can elaborate on this wrap by
adding more hearts, in red velvet or gold foil, so
that your country look becomes more Victorian.
Try putting a tiny cloth rose at the heart of each
bow. Just remember that the theme of Valentine's
Day is love, so anything that suggests romance is
more than appropriate.

Wedding wraps do not have to be formal white and silver creations anymore. This wonderful wrap brings a breath of fresh air to a traditional occasion. However, because the spray of flowers used is made up of fresh wildflowers, the life expectancy of the wrap is only a day, if that. You can use this "fresh flower" approach to wrapping a thank-you gift, or any spontaneous little present.

Wrap the gift in a paper with an understated pattern. Do not pick a paper that will compete with the bouquet. This paper, for example, uses only two colors, both of which are muted enough to complement the natural beauty of the flowers.

Make a small bouquet. This bouquet uses daisies and white spray foliage held together, literally and figuratively, by wire stems threaded with tiny fake pearls, which you can buy at a good craft store. When you are satisfied with the arrangement, wrap the wire around the stems to hold everything in place. Then, fold a piece of paper towel and dampen it to wrap around the flower stems. Cut down a small plastic sandwich bag and put the wrapped bouquet base in the bag. Secure the bag around the stems with a rubber band. Cut off any excess plastic above the rubber band.

Make a cone from a paper doily. Slip the bouquet into the cone. Adjust the cone until you have a snug fit and tape it together. Then, lay the cone, with the bouquet inside, on the gift. Attach the doily to the package with double-sided tape. Use a length of satin cloth ribbon to make a bow. Tie the ribbon reasonably tightly around the gift to further secure the bouquet, and—quick!—run, do not walk, to the wedding!

he frothiness of this wedding wrap combines the delicacy of a silk flower bow with flowered paper, tulle, and six stems of wired pearls. Roses, symbols of love and fidelity, are repeated throughout the wrap. This is the kind of wrap that deserves to sit, unopened, on a receiving table.

You will need, in addition to the paper (make sure you buy extra for the "fan"), 2 yards (1¾ meters) of tulle (available at fabric stores), wired pearls (available at crafts stores), and a single silk rose from the florist. You should also have an artist's compass on hand.

Use a paper that is patterned with roses or some other real flower to coordinate especially well with your bow. Wrap the present with the Seamless Wrap (see page 12).

To create a raised background for your rose, use the compass to draw a circle with a 2-inch (5-centimeter) radius on the wrong side of the wrapping paper. Cut it out. Cut one quarter of the circle away in the shape of a large pie slice. Then, fold the remaining three-quarter circle, accordion style. The folds should be about a ½-inch (1¼ centimeters) apart. Put this aside.

Scrunch up the tulle and use it as a ribbon, wrapped asymmetrically around the package. Make a conventional bow with the tulle on the package top and fluff out the ends. Make a small spray from the wired pearls and push the ends into the knot of the tulle bow, which will hold them in place. If necessary, fan the pearls out further once they are in place. Now add the silk rose, pushing its stem into the tulle knot, as well. Finally, unfold the three-quarter paper circle and place it, fan-like, up against the back of the bow. The fan acts as a backdrop, but you may find that you have to cut a circle out of the fan center to fit it around the bow. Trim and adjust until everything is just right.

When you are satisfied with the look, staple the fan to itself where it meets and crosses behind and around the bow. If you need to, carefully tape the fan to the package, too. This will hold the fan up and in the correct shape.

W

hen you have
to do an unexpected wrap job, and you think
you have no materials in the house—do not
panic! You probably have just what you need to
make this eye-catching, springtime wrap. All you
need are scraps of bright paper, both plain and
patterned if you like, a snippet of ribbon, glue,
and a sheet of matte paper.

Wrap the gift using the Seamless Wrap (see
page 12). Take the longest scrap you have and
make it into a paper "ribbon" by cutting a rectangle that is double the width of the box depth
and 2½ times the length of the box. Fold the
rectangle lengthwise in half. Stick the folded rectangle to the wrapped box about an inch (2½
centimeters) away from the edge of one of the
long sides. Loop it all the way around the box as if
it were a ribbon, and tape it down with double-
faced tape.

Tear pieces of paper into various small shapes
and experiment on the box before you start to
stick anything down. Do you want to make a
garden scene? a bouquet? An animal?

When you have composed your picture, stick
the pieces down with a little white glue. Then
make a small bow from a ribbon fragment, if you
have one, and stick it on the paper "ribbon." An
absolutely original wrap design!

To construct a paper-covered keepsake house box, you will need a 36-inch (91-centimeter) square of ¼-inch (⅗-centimeter) foam board (available at framing, crafts, and art supply stores), an art knife, white glue, a medium stiff-bristled brush, pencil, ruler, and a ½-yard (45 centimeters) of wrapping paper.

Foam board is easy to cut and provides a sturdy base for constructing this box. It is easier to work with than cardboard, and is readily available at crafts stores. Perhaps the most critical factor in building a sturdy house is measuring accurately with a ruler. And since your knife blade will be very sharp, remember to lay down a piece of cardboard before cutting, to shield your work surface.

To make a basic house box, begin by measuring a 6-by-10-inch (15¼-by-25-centimeter) piece of foam board for the base. Cut it out by placing the ruler against the line to be cut, and drawing the knife blade down along the edge of the ruler with a moderate amount of pressure. Repeat if necessary to cut all the way through the foam board. Measure and cut out two more rectangles, 6¼-by-9½ inches (16-by-24 centimeters) each, to form the unpeaked sides.

To form the peaked sides, measure and cut out two more rectangles, 6-by-10¼ inches (15¼-by-26 centimeters) each. To make the peaks, measure and mark two points along the edge of each long side of the rectangles, 4¼ inches (10¾ centimeters) from the top. Then mark the center point of the top edge, and draw two straight lines connecting it to the points on the sides. Cut away the corners along the lines you have drawn. Repeat with the other 6-by-10¼-inch (15¼-by-26-centimeter) rectangle. Now you are ready to assemble the house.

Place the base piece flat upon the work surface. Brush a thin line of glue along the edge of one of the short sides. Then take one of the peaked ends and press its flat edge against the line of glue so that the two pieces are at a 90-degree angle. Either hold in place by hand during the next step, or insert a straight pin to keep the walls steady. Use the same method to glue one of the 6¼-by-9½-inch (16-by-24-centimeter) pieces in place, next to the peaked side, to form a corner. Repeat the process until each side has been glued to the base and the adjoining sides.

Allow your project to dry for at least a half hour before continuing.

To make the roof, measure a piece of foam board 10-by-10 inches (25-by-25 centimeters) and cut it out. Score it lightly down the center line with your knife, making a slit that does not go all the way through the foam board. Bend the roof piece in half along the scored line, and determine how much it has to be bent to form the roof by fitting it gently on the base.

To cover the box with paper, first make sure all glue is completely dry. Then cut a piece of paper measuring 12-by-36 inches (30-by-91 centimeters). Brush an even coat of glue all over one of the peaked sides. Place the paper face down on the work surface. With a ¼-inch (⅗-centimeter) margin of paper at the edge, lay the peaked side down on the paper, leaving a 1-inch (2½-centimeter) overhang of paper on both the top and

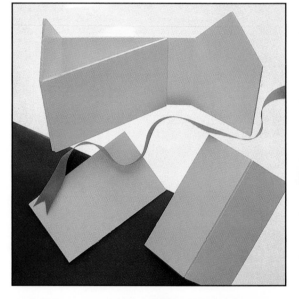

bottom edge of the foam board. Smooth out all wrinkles.

Brush glue evenly on the next side of the house, and turn the house over on the paper, so that the side with the glue is against it. Pull the paper taut, and smooth out any wrinkles. Repeat the process with the third side. Before you secure that last side, however, stretch the ¼-inch (⅗-centimeter) overlap from the beginning of the paper around the corner to the uncovered side and glue it down. Then fold the side edge under to make a "hem," and glue the last side down in the same manner as the other sides. Fold the remaining inch (2½ centimeters) of paper hanging from the bottom edge of the box underneath the box, slitting it diagonally at the corners if necessary to make the folding easier. Glue it down underneath the box.

Trim the excess paper on the top edge to within 1 inch (2½ centimeters) of the edge, fold it over the rim of the box, slitting it diagonally at the corners if necessary, and glue it to the inside of the box.

To cover the roof, measure and cut out a 13-by-13-inch (33-by-33-centimeter) square of paper. Keeping the roof piece bent at the correct angle at all times, brush the roof piece with glue, center the paper over it and press it down, smoothing out any wrinkles. Fold over any excess paper, and glue it to the underside of the roof. The last step is to set the roof on the base and tie a securing ribbon around the two parts.

The abundance of the harvest season is wonderfully reflected in this earthy wrap. Use it for a Thanksgiving gift, or as a birthday wrap for anyone you know who has an autumn birthday.

Go to a farmer's market or a florist and buy grapevine. Ideally, you should get this from your garden so that you can be sure the vine is flexible and fresh, but not all of us can do this! Also buy a small bare twig wreath, and some small, colorful dried flowers.

Wrap your gift with glossy red paper, using the Seamless Wrap (see page 12). Twist the grapevine around the wrapped box, weaving the stalks in and out of themselves. The rustic feel of this wrap means that you do not have to worry about "perfection"; the unexpected weave of the wrap is its charm, so go ahead and twist, wind and snap the branches as needed, but just be a little careful not to break the vine. The tension of the branches will hold them around the box, so you do not have to worry about secretly attaching the twigs to the box. If you are uneasy about the vine staying in precise position, you can cheat with a little florist's wire.

Glue—sparingly!—the dried flowers one by one onto the small wreath. Try to cluster them a little bit to give an abundant look and to create a burst of color against the red backdrop.

When you have decorated the wreath to your liking, attach it to your wrap with a tiny piece of ribbon, tied in a double bow, that picks up the wrap color. Wind the ribbon twice around the wreath, then weave it through the twigs and tie. To stop the wreath from flopping against the wrap, use two or three very small pieces of double-sided tape to stick it to the paper.

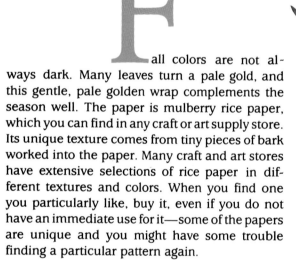

Fall colors are not always dark. Many leaves turn a pale gold, and this gentle, pale golden wrap complements the season well. The paper is mulberry rice paper, which you can find in any craft or art supply store. Its unique texture comes from tiny pieces of bark worked into the paper. Many craft and art stores have extensive selections of rice paper in different textures and colors. When you find one you particularly like, buy it, even if you do not have an immediate use for it—some of the papers are unique and you might have some trouble finding a particular pattern again.

The ribbon is a natural fiber ribbon, also purchased from a craft store. About 3 yards (2¾ meters) of ribbon should see you through this complete bow. Begin by wrapping the fiber twice around the package from top to bottom. Tie a conventional bow at the package top. Pull the loops apart slightly on the package for an unusual touch. Find a leaf that captures the feeling of fall—in color, shape, and texture—and gently stick it to the box edge at the top, next to the bow, using double-sided tape. Next, stick a pinecone on top of the leaf with a tiny spot of glue. Even after the glue has dried, this wrap will never be absolutely firm. So, if you are thinking of practicing a few football passes with this gift—do not.

Christmas' magical glitter and shine are brought out in this startling wrap. Start with glossy, deep blue paper for a Seamless Wrap (see page 12). Use a tree tinsel garland for a ribbon, plucking out strands if you think the look is too full. The "bow" on this package comes in two parts. The first is a conventional bow tied with the tinsel. The second part is made from three clear glass tree ornaments (available in the holiday section of a department or variety store) stuffed with opalescent cellophane. Cut strips of cellophane and push them into the ornaments until they are as full as you wish. Then tie these to the wrap at the center of the tinsel bow.

The crowning touch of the wrap is three Christmas icicles, probably available where you bought the glass ornaments. Tie these to the center of the bow and arrange them in a cluster, to act as frosty exclamation points on your wrap.

There is no reason why a wrapped wine or champagne bottle has to look <u>exactly</u> like what it is. With some ingenuity, you can camouflage the bottle a little.

Lay a length of wrapping paper face down and place the bottle 1 inch (2 ½ centimeters) from the bottom. With a piece of tape, anchor the bottle against one edge of the paper, making sure *not* to tape the bottle's label. Roll it up and close the bottom by folding the bottom edges under. Leave the top end open and standing straight up. In the Christmas ornaments section of a department store or variety store, collect a selection of three different sizes of gold, ball tree ornaments. Also buy a couple of flat golden ornaments to act as backdrops for the gold balls. Your next stop is the florist, where you should buy some greens and some florist's wire.

Arrange the gold balls and flat ornaments so that they form a semicircular, arced bouquet. Hold them together at their bases with the florist's wire. Then add the greens to the back of the balls and ornaments. Attach with more wire. Finally, just push the base of the bouquet into the space left between the bottle neck and the paper wall. Use tissue paper in the remaining space around the bottle neck to support the bouquet. Try to set the arrangement at an angle, so that it looks as if it is about to slide down the side of the bottle. When you are satisfied with the placement of the crown, move down the bottle and stick stars haphazardly on the paper. Finish off the wrap with a traditional red cloth ribbon and bow at the bottle center. (Do not forget to notch the ribbon ends.) Now, who could guess what all this finery conceals?

We all associate music with Christmas—whether it is carols or Handel's "Messiah." Use these motifs to make a lovely, musical Christmas wrap for your favorite musician or music lover.

Start with a piece of sheet music, which you can buy at music stores. Or, go to the library and photocopy the music for a carol or the Halleluiah Chorus. Wrap the gift with a Seamless Wrap (see page 12), using the sheet music. Tie a huge, red moiré cloth ribbon around the wrapped box, bringing the ends together with a slip knot. The opulent look of this wrapped gift is best created with a ribbon that is a full third the width of one big box side.

Leave the knot loose. In the Christmas ornament section of a department store or specialty store, look for gold painted plastic horns and trumpets—or, failing that, toy horns that you can spray paint gold. Buy plastic cranberry sprigs, too. At the florist, pick up some greens and wire.

Push the necks of the horns into the loose knot of the bow on your package. Attach the cranberries with the wire and tighten the knot. Slide the greens in between the ribbon and the paper. A gift to inspire song!

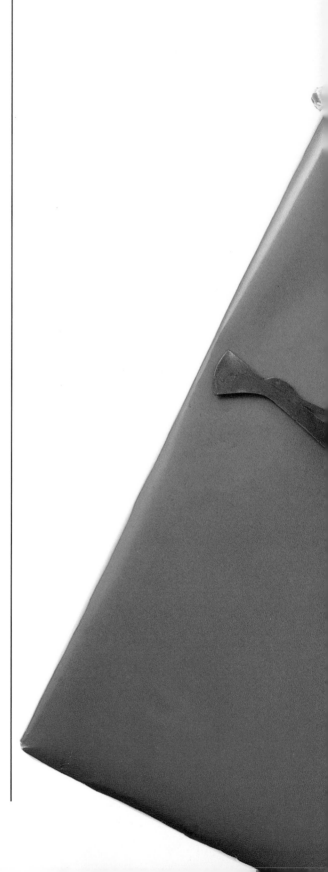

This rich, glossy green paper is the perfect foil for a heralding angel. The angel in the photograph was a one-time find in a flea market, but you can find your own special angel simply by browsing through flea markets and out-of-the-way antique stores. Try to use something that has a hole or loop for easy attachment to a ribbon or wrap in some way, so you can achieve this same dangling, tree ornament look.

Begin with a Seamless Wrap (see page 12). Then, using multicolored silk cording from a fabric store, tie a bow near the box top, looping the cord only once around the package. The ribbon—or, in this case, bar—attached to the ornament should be included in the knot of the bow. If this will make the knot too bulky, slip the bar (or ribbon) through the knot and secure it above by incorporating it into the tied bouquet of greens. Then fill out the greens with white flowered sprigs, and add a touch of whimsy with a golden star at the end of one of the silken cords—the Christmas star, perhaps?

SOMETHING SPECTACULAR · 113

A cheeky, black wooden Scottie peeking out from behind a tartan ribbon is a surprise—and a delight! You can find silhouetted shapes such as this in better department stores, pet stores, and toy stores. Wrap a gift with shiny red paper and make a conventional cross bow from cloth tartan ribbon, bought in a fabric store. Use wide ribbon, for impact and texture. Notch the ribbon ends to prevent fraying, and slip the dog in between the package and the ribbon. Use two small pieces of double-sided tape to prevent the dog from slipping. This basic idea can be varied endlessly; any flat form will lend itself to this sort of wrap.

ways seems to be a problem. Cookies usually get wrapped in tins or aluminum foil. Most other homemade foods end up arriving in their birthday suits, or on a plate that has to be returned. But there is a solution! Most department stores now have cookware departments that cater to gourmet cooks. These stores now carry the small cardboard containers that we have always associated with take-out Chinese foods. A number of specialty mail-order houses, such as Williams Sonoma, offer the same items. Try raiding the box selections of good card stores, too. You can personalize these anonymous little containers with magic markers, ribbons, and stick-ons. Also try tearing up colored papers, as you did with the springtime wrap, and sticking them down with white glue. Steer clear of paint, though, because you do not want to run the risk of the paint seeping into the food.

Many houseware stores now stock specialty boxes. This bonbon-style box can be purchased in just such a store, then stuffed with homemade sweets or tiny cookies. Roll them up first in colored tissue paper for protection, and then put them in the box. Make sure the tissue paper sticks out of the ends enticingly. Crimp the ends and tie them with ribbon. A mouthwatering gift!

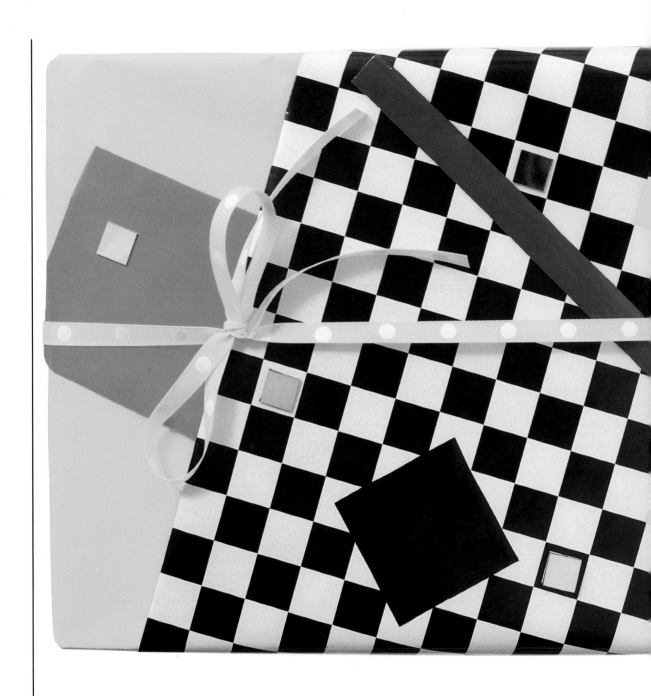

When you have almost run out of paper, and you have to wrap something fast, there is only one solution—use patchwork! This wrap was based on the remains of a sheet of yellow wrapping paper that did not quite make it all the way around—so the seam was placed in the middle of the box top. The gaps were hidden with a sheet of contrasting leftover paper that was such an awkward shape it could only have been used to wrap a set of knitting needles or chopsticks.

Wrap your gift as best you can, using the Seamless Wrap technique. Use tiny bits of transparent tape to stick the paper to the box. Establish the problem areas you want to hide, and go to town with scraps of wrapping paper. Stick down paper shapes anywhere you want, trying, if possible, to keep within reasonable color limitations. Use glue and double-sided tape, depending on the size of the piece of paper (the smaller the scrap, the better glue works). Pull the look together with a ribbon that picks up colors you have used—in this case, yellow. Each patchwork wrap is a unique creation, and you may even want to try it for fun, not just because you have run out of paper and cannot do anything else.

Truly odd-shaped packages no longer have to baffle the wrapper. When you wrap a long, slim box, try sticking two sheets of paper together and using them as if they were one. This gift was wrapped with two papers that are similar in color schemes and patterns, but are still obviously different. A third paper was fashioned into a surprising bow that hides the seam and holds the look together.

Attach the two sheets of paper along their shorter sides with transparent tape and wrap your gift, using a Seamless Wrap (see page 12). Make sure the seam of the two papers is in the center of the package.

When the box is wrapped, take the third paper and measure two bands that will go around the box middle. Calculate the length of these bands by measuring twice the package width, plus twice the package depth, plus 1 inch (2½ centimeters). Also, make the band twice the width you will need. Cut out the bands. Fold one band's long raw edges under the whole length of the strip so they meet in the center of the band back. This way no raw edges will show on the package.

Stick that band around the box middle, using double-sided tape under the band and transparent tape on the package back where the band ends overlap.

Take the second paper band and fold the edges under as you did with the first, but this time use transparent tape to seal the center seam where the raw edges meet on the back of this strip, since you will be tying this length of "ribbon" in a knot. Fold over and tape down the raw edges of the short ends as well. Slip this long strip under the first band and very carefully tie a conventional knot. Do not pull it tight. Just pull it to the point where its own tension holds it. Be sure you tie the knot with the seam side down. And there you have a wrap to solve any lengthy problem.

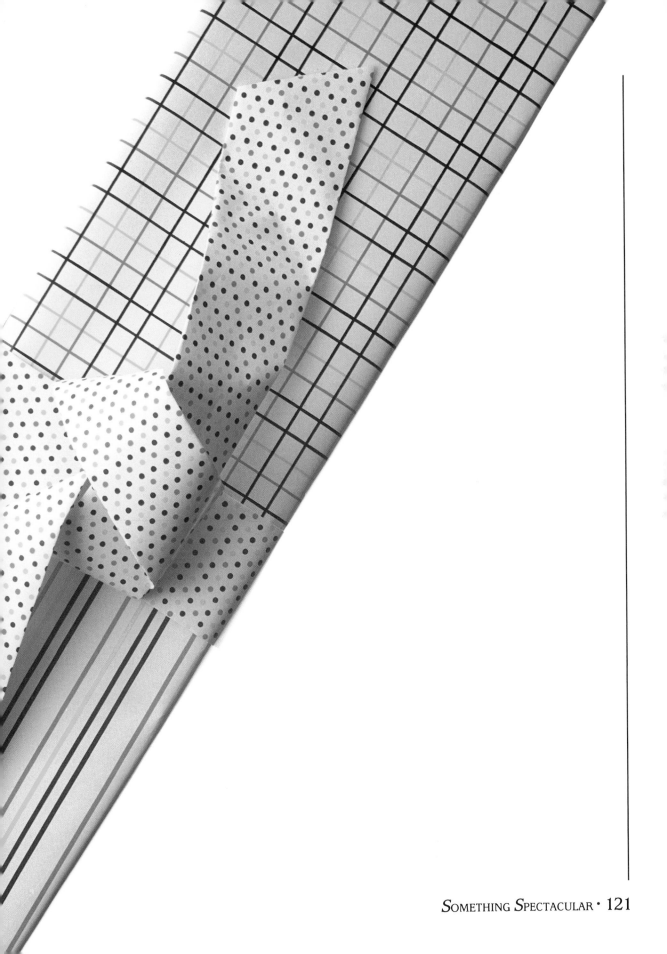

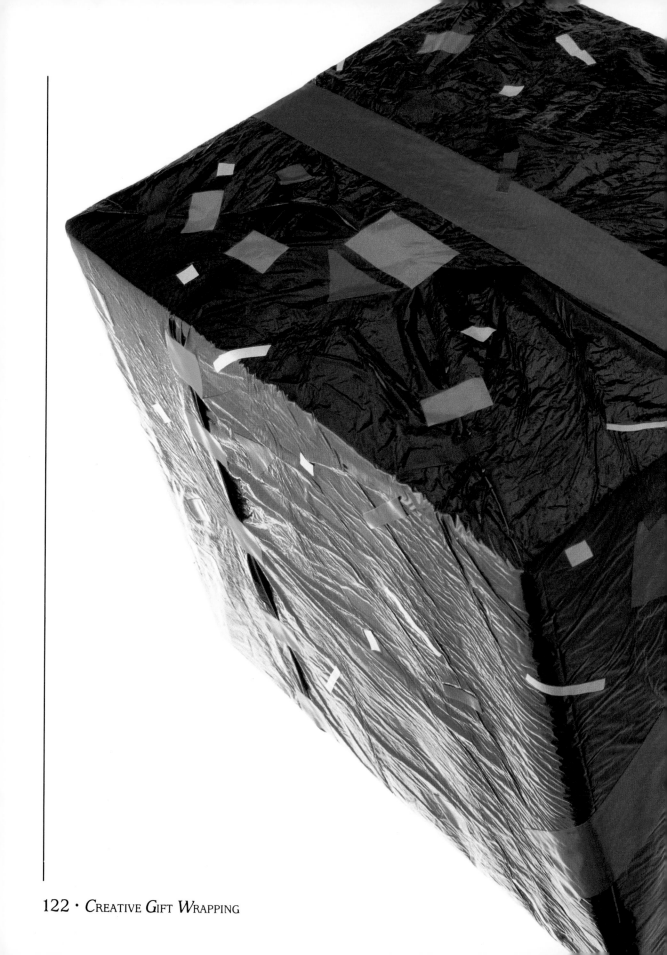

G iving a huge present like a washing machine usually means sticking a bow somewhere on the unwrapped present—no prize for guessing what the bow hides! Try going one step beyond basic by experimenting with plastic garbage bags and colorful electrical tape (purchased at any hardware store). Use the tape on the seams, and just as decoration. Be careful, however, not to let the tape come in contact with the surface of the present, since it can be annoyingly tenacious.

S ome gifts have a short life. Yet the memory of their thoughtfulness remains. When giving plants or flowers, it is so much nicer to place them in a beautiful container that will camouflage the plastic pot. An inexpensive basket shields the pot yet allows the plant to be watered. Adding two wooden, brightly painted miniature houses, perhaps with the name of the recipient inscribed on the sides, provides an additional element which expresses your creativity and care.

For this special wrap, you will need a plastic pot liner that will fit over the plastic pot the plant comes in, a larger basket or other decorative container, sheet moss (optional), ribbon, two miniature wooden houses, and two small eye hooks.

Place the pot liner into the basket and then place the potted plant in the liner.

If everything does not fit flush exactly, or you want to conceal the liner and plastic pot, simply cut some sheet moss to fit around the base of the plant and tuck it into the basket.

Screw the hook eyes into the tops of the miniature houses and string some ribbon through the eyes. Then tie the houses to the handle of the basket and end off the ribbon in a simple bow.

Sources

If you were to ask where to purchase gift wrapping supplies, the overwhelming answer would be, "Everywhere!" The vast variety of shops that handle paper and ribbon products range from signature-card and party shops to department stores and five-and-dimes. And, at the ever increasing number of open-air markets and antique shops, you can often find country-style papers and decorative bags for sale.

Other alternatives are mail-order catalogs, and school, church, and civic organizations, which sometimes sell gift wrapping accessories as fund-raising events.

In addition, single-sheet specialty paper—marbleized, rice, Mylar—and handmade papers are available through art supply stores and certain crafts shops. Ribbons can be found by the yard at craft and fabric stores, sewing centers, and florist shops, as well as through mail-order sources. Ribbon by the yard allows you the freedom of expanding the standard ribbon treatment into a personalized creation. Your local florist will also have a number of little decorative objects just right for adding onto your packages, as well as a fresh flower to grace the package top.

Balloon City, USA
P.O. Box 1445
Harrisburg, PA 17105-1445

Fiber Craft Materials
Kirchen Brothers
P.O. Box 1016
Skokie, IL 60076

Hallmark Cards
25th and McGee
Kansas City, MO 64108

Hurley Patentee Manor
RD #7
P.O. Box 98A
Kingston, NY 12401
914-331-5414

Ribbons by Offray Ribbon Company
C.M. Offray & Son, Inc.
Rt. 24
P.O. Box 601
Chester, NJ 07930-0601

Ribbon Narrow Fiber Company, Inc.
565 Windsor Drive
Secaucus, NJ 07094

The Stephen Lawrence Company.
450 Commerce Road
Carlstadt, NJ 07072

INDEX